T0205117

JOURNEY

I, WITNESS

JOURNEY

My Story of Migration

LUIS ONOFRE VALENCIA

Norton Young Readers

An Imprint of W. W. Norton & Company
Independent Publishers Since 1923

Series edited by Anika Hussain, Amanda Uhle, and Dave Eggers

Copyright © 2024 by The Hawkins Project and Luis Onofre Valencia

For information about permission to reproduce selections from this book, write to
Permissions, W. W. Norton & Company, Inc., 500 Fifth Avenue, New York, NY 10110

For information about special discounts for bulk purchases, please contact
W. W. Norton Special Sales at specialsales@wwnorton.com or 800-233-4830

Manufacturing by Lake Book Manufacturing
Book design by Hana Anouk Nakamura
Production manager: Delaney Adams

ISBN 978-1-324-05231-9

W. W. Norton & Company, Inc., 500 Fifth Avenue, New York, N.Y. 10110
www.wwnorton.com

W. W. Norton & Company Ltd., 15 Carlisle Street, London W1D 3BS

1 2 3 4 5 6 7 8 9 0

This book is dedicated to anyone who has made the same journey, the invisible working class, those who feel lost between two cultures, and to the youth with big emotions and very few ways to express them. I see you.

"Let them see my weakness, and let them see me overcome it."

—Brandon Sanderson

CONTENTS

INTRODUCTION

Anika Hussein and Amanda Uhle

One of the best ways to understand other people's struggles and achievements is to read their personal stories. That's what this series is all about: letting young people share their own experiences. As series editors, our hope is that by hearing one person's story, our readers will learn more about the complex world we all inhabit together and think of ways we might make it more peaceful and equitable.

Teenagers like Malala Yousafzai and Greta Thunberg became iconic for standing up for what they believe is right. Other teens, not yet as well known, have also stepped up to make a difference. When Adama Bah was a teenager in post-9/11 New York, she was falsely accused of being a terrorist simply because she is Muslim. She spoke up to defend herself and others like her. When Salvador Gómez-Colón was fifteen, his family endured Hurricane Maria in Puerto Rico. Using his deep local knowledge and incredible dedication to helping his neighbors, Salvador founded Light and Hope for Puerto Rico, raising money and gathering supplies to help islanders with basic needs during the emergency.

The I, Witness books bring you stories of young people like you who have faced extraordinary challenges in their lives. Their stories are exciting and surprising, filled with struggle—and humor and joy, too. We hope that you'll consider your own life and your own story as you read. Is there a problem in the world or in your life that you'd like to help solve?

In this book, you'll meet Luis Onofre Valencia, who was born in Mexico and traveled to California as a young child without legal documentation. Luis and his family members crossed the United States' southern border in separate trips, and they faced danger and uncertainty on their journey. Once they arrived, they faced other dangers and other uncertainties as they navigated the immigration system, learned a new language, and acclimated to American culture. As Luis worked to fit in at his school and in his neighborhood, both he and his brother also grappled with their own mental health, and their family continued to seek stable housing. Luis survived with support from caring adults in his life, especially Coach McCarthy, who became an important part of Luis's health and well-being when he became a high school student-athlete wrestler. Luis then went on to become a celebrated NAIA and NCAA Division II wrestler in college. Now that he's an adult, Luis supports vulnerable people through his work as a therapist with

San Francisco's Street Crisis Response Team, which works to resolve difficult situations before involving the police. He still wrestles today and is also a part-time coach.

Many of us will recognize the trials Luis has faced, and all of us will be moved by his determination in the face of horrific challenges and the incredible empathy that he brings to his work as an activist today. As readers ourselves, we were heartened and inspired by Luis's story, and hope you will be, too.

JOURNEY

CHAPTER 1

Community

"**Sueltame!**" My voice trembled and cracked as I pleaded. I looked around, tears welling in my eyes, hoping to catch the sympathy of one of my vecinos as I begged Mama to let go of my arm. My cries were drowned out as dozens of vendors encouraged passersby to step right up to their colorful booths.

Mama held on, calmly enduring my tantrum, waiting for the storm to tire itself out and move on. In my peaceful town in the state of Michoacán, the tianguis—flea market—was one of my favorite places to be. Hundreds of vendors would flood the streets and sell . . . well, everything. There were tools and toys, beds and bread. There were performances, from lucha to live music, and pockets of fruity, spicy, or practically any other delicious scent you could think of. As a five-year-old boy, this magical place would light a fire in my belly and I'd ping-pong all around, making

Mama chase me for hours. I'll be honest, it wasn't easy for her when I ran through the streets. Things would spill. I was in danger of getting lost. But today she had trapped me. Sure, I whined when she bought me colorful leather huaraches, and protested that I didn't get my wrestling action figure, but deep down I was actually upset with her for outsmarting me. She really pulled the damage control card and decided to take me to the tianguis only if I held her hand the entire time.

"Ahora que tiene el bebe?" My older sisters said in unison, teasing as they referred to me as a baby. Isabel and Joanna ran by, their hair clips bouncing rhythmically. I flung my leg at them, but I was caught by the anchor of Mama's grip and missed widely. I lost my balance and fell to the ground in an embarrassing one-two combo. Mama caught me, though. I tried my hardest to annoy her again and made my body as heavy as I could. Mama let out a melodic laugh, her gentle eyes not a match for her strong grip, and teased me by sticking out her tongue. I tried my hardest not to echo her laughter, but moments later my pouty mask fell apart.

"Niño guerroso!" Mama said, hauling me up, calling me a pain in an endearing way.

**

Mama and I made our way back to our neighborhood, passing through the plaza, exchanging hearty greetings with several of the townsfolk. Across from the statue of the Tlahualil, an Aztec warrior, Mama stopped to talk with Chavo, Papa's younger cousin. He talked to Mama about a few of his friends, now deemed "Norteamericanos," who went up north to the United States for a few years and came back flaunting new cars, gold chains, and nice dress clothes. As if manifested through our conversation, a sleek crimson '94 Pontiac Grand Prix slowly drove by us, blasting music. The three of us made eye contact with the driver, who gave us a side smirk.

"I bet you anything we just made that guy's day," Mama said slyly. Chavo ignored her, though, and continued to stare.

"Can you imagine how marvelous it is up there?" Chavo said, in a trance. "My cousin told me they practically sweep up money in the north."

Mama let out a stiff laugh and shook her head. "Don't fall for that fantasy. I hear there's work at the Coca-Cola factory in Jiquilpan," she stated.

Chavo sighed.

"I would rather they pay me a full dollar than a fraction of one," he grumbled. We said goodbye and Mama wished him luck.

"Que estes bien," she said, "Échale

muchas ganas." She wished him well and to show lots of effort.

As we continued our walk, we saw the red Pontiac again. Mama called the driver a "cangrejo" under her breath. A crab? Unsure of what she meant, I asked her to clarify. Mama laughed with a distinct tone of embarrassment.

"Well, you know how crabs pull each other down when they get caught in buckets so they all suffer together?" I shook my head, unsure of what she meant. "I'll tell you about debt when you're older," she said.

**

We arrived at my papa's corner market, a convenience store he had inherited from his former boss, who had passed away a few years prior. The store did well, despite a larger market just a few blocks away. Papa worked pretty much every day, sunrise to sunset. After school, my siblings would help with tasks. My sister Isabel and brother Hector would help with deliveries, handling cutlery, and anything that required math. My other siblings, my sister Joanna and my brother Mateo, would assist Papa with cleaning, restocking, and cashier duties. As the baby, I wasn't allowed to help yet, though I would often imitate tianguis vendors.

"Páse, primo," I would say, inviting folks in as they passed by.

Toward the end of the day, Papa asked me to hand him the mail. He froze at the sight of a big envelope. I stared as he read, his smile slowly withering. I asked him what was wrong, and he told me, "Nothing, mijo."

That evening, I overheard Papa whispering to Mama.

"We're getting shut down," he said.

CHAPTER 2

Separation

My tia Victoria's house was always jam-packed for our usual Sunday get-together. This week we were watching World Cup playoff action, despite Mexico losing in the previous round. The house smelled amazing, as my tia had made manchamantel, a delicious dish usually reserved for special occasions. I tried to dip my finger in the mixture of poultry, mole, and spices, but Papa scooped me up and took me out into the backyard to join the rest of my family.

Despite the high-spirited nature of the game, there seemed to be a mournful energy enveloping our usual celebration. My eyes settled on my older brother Mateo, and I could tell he'd been crying. Soon Papa told me that he loved me and wanted to do everything he could for me and my siblings. Our eyes met and he whispered to me that he had to go away for a while. A note of sadness rippled across my body, like a guitar chord, strumming with every heartbeat. I wasn't surprised: his store had shut down a few months before.

"Are you okay?" he asked.

"Yes," I lied.

He put me down slowly and I excused myself. As soon as I was out of sight, I ran up the stairs to my cousin's bedroom and slammed the door behind me. With my back against the wall, I sank down to the floor.

"Ahora que tiene el bebe?" My older brother Hector's voice startled me. We made eye contact, his boyish stubble highlighted by the blue glow of the TV. I heard a faint whisper inside my head, a distant thought at first. It grew louder the more I paid attention to it. I approached the abnormal thoughts with curiosity, mindful of their existence though I knew not to listen to them.

Papa is leaving us.

Papa doesn't love us.

Papa is abandoning us.

With the thoughts, I heard also the imaginary words of Joselito, the legendary boy-hero of my hometown. His voice helped me reframe my negative thoughts, comforting me as my mind became my biggest enemy. It was a trick that Mama taught me.

Papa is making a sacrifice for us.

He's leaving to provide for us.

He loves us so much.

As if noticing the desert of thoughts I'd

lost myself in, Hector invited me over to sit with him. He cradled me in his lap.

"He'll be back," Hector told me, unpausing his game of *The Death and Return of Superman*. As I watched the comic-panel-style scenes, I was moved by the story of the hero of Metropolis, a righteous man who went to a strange world. My eyelids grew heavy and my body melted onto my brother's. Before I drifted off to sleep, I was convinced that Papa and Superman were one and the same.

**

"Technically, you have the most important job," Joanna said as she gripped the steering wheel of her toy jeep. Mateo revved the engine of his twin white jeep, the gentle hum of the battery urging me to the starting line. We were up on the roof, three stories above ground.

I sighed out loud and reluctantly picked up the white flag yet again.

"Okay, but I get the next race," I said. "Ready?"

The two crouched over their steering wheels, waiting for their cue. I lifted the white flag in the air, but was momentarily distracted by the mailman across the road. Mateo was the second to spot him. It had been a few months since Papa went up north, and I missed him a great deal. He used to call every day, then every other day. Lately, he hadn't been calling, but he continued to send money to us. Deep down, I thought it was my fault somehow, and his departure would replay sadly in my mind.

"Cartero!" Mateo called out to the mailman. "Don't forget to bring us a letter from Papa."

I felt a painful strum flow through my body, and I dropped the white flag. Joanna's jeep shot forward like a rocket. Mateo jumped in surprise and slammed his foot on the accelerator a moment later. As the two toy jeeps raced through the third-story roof, I shook off my momentary feelings of guilt and chased after my siblings, cutting across the glass skylight. I heard a slight crack under my foot. Hector looked up from his book and frowned at me.

"Luis," he said, "I told you not to step on that."

Since Papa left, my big brother had changed, acting as if he were our father. I decided to challenge him that day.

I smirked and pressed my foot against the glass. It shattered and I fell through.

The recovery process wasn't as bad as I had imagined. I got a cool-looking scar on my leg and time on our Super Nintendo. The plunge, however, had left some invisible scars inside me. The three-second mental loop of falling through the glass joined the one of my father leaving to go up north and haunted me.

One morning a little while after the accident, after a few weeks of not hearing from Papa, I woke up from a dream and looked to my left. It was five forty-five and Mateo was already getting out of bed. He'd gotten good at maintaining this routine. He quietly crossed the bedroom, and I hurried after him. I didn't intend to let him leave me behind this time.

We arrived at the post office hand in hand. The two of us stood and asked every mailman if he had a letter from our papa. The pitying looks they gave conveyed more than words could.

We went home with our hands empty, and Mateo hurried to school. Left all by myself, my intrusive thoughts pressed into my brain.

He's had enough of you.

It's your fault he hasn't called.

Your behavior caused this, and he stopped loving you.

The thoughts were harder to reframe this time, but Joselito's voice still came.

Papa is busy.

He will never stop loving you.

He will write when he can.

That evening we finally received a phone call from Papa. He apologized for his silence—he'd been traveling down to Southern California. He said he had exciting news, and Mama, my siblings, and I all huddled around the phone.

"I want us all to be together more than anything," he said. "I've arranged for you all to join me here in the U.S."

We were stunned, but I was so excited to be reunited with him. After we hung up, we all agreed we would make the journey up north. We were buzzing with anticipation.

"God bless America," Mateo said, showing off his English lessons, and we laughed.

We would finally all be together, as a family.

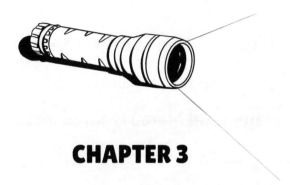

CHAPTER 3

Crossing

The news of reuniting with Papa in an entirely different world struck me with excitement and wonder. A new life in the United States, home of bald eagles, the New York Yankees, and Hollywood. We would be practically sweeping up money, I fantasized. The three youngest of us, Mateo, Joanna, and I, quickly leaned heavily in favor of the prospect of a new life elsewhere.

Joanna and Mateo enjoyed messing with their gullible youngest brother by playing with the thoughts in my head about the journey. They told me tall tales of coyotes speaking Spanish and guiding people across the border into the U.S. I became anxious about our journey and these strange creatures.

It all happened quickly. Suddenly family and friends were coming by to wish us well. Our goodbye celebration was mournful despite amazing food and company. When the sun set we all gathered outside and sang folk songs. My big sister Isabel strummed the guitar and everyone followed along in her rendition of "Caminos de Michoacán," a song about traveling through the state that we all loved. I'd never understood its message until that moment, when I was about to leave Michoacán.

Finally, one evening, my siblings and I packed into the back of a pickup, with Mama at the wheel. I kissed my cousins and tias goodbye. As we drove away, I watched my loved ones and everything I'd known drift further and further away, until they disappeared into the night. It felt like a dagger was piercing my heart.

***

Tijuana would be where my family parted ways for the first time. The plan was that the two youngest, Mateo and I, would cross with the documents of our U.S.-born cousins, while the rest would go on foot. Only later would I learn details of their harrowing journey.

We left most of our possessions behind, but Mama brought with her a single crucifix blessed by a priest, to guide us safely through our journey. Upon arriving at Tijuana, we all held each other tightly and said we'd see each other soon. My cousins Angela and Mario waited patiently in their truck. I was scared, but Mama bent down to my eye level, and I could see the moonlight reflected on her rosary necklace. She lifted it over her head and placed it around my neck. "This will protect you," she said. "You'll be safe."

"You promise?" I asked.

Mateo stepped in and echoed her. I felt better with his comfort, and promised to be strong.

Then Mama and the rest of my family were gone.

Mateo and I climbed onto the front seat, my eyes wide and my lips quivering. My body couldn't digest what was happening. I was alert and wide awake, despite the night sky above us. The drive to the border was torturous and overstimulating. We shared ghost stories, including the legend of the nagual, a strange creature that had the ability to shapeshift. I began to panic, fear overtaking me. I could only focus on my racing thoughts, which grew louder and louder.

I can't do this.

We're going to get caught.

I'm too stupid to pull this off.

The guards will know I'm lying.

I'm going to ruin it for everyone.

I'm not smart enough.

I'm going to fail.

Deep down I heard a faint whisper

telling me not to listen to those thoughts, though it was very distant and hard to hear. I whimpered and Mateo squeezed my hand, grounding me. I felt my panic ease.

The border gates stretched into the sky. A line of cars was slowly swallowed by the gaping mouth of the gate. The blinding headlights at the very top resembled two evil eyes, constantly on the lookout. Faceless guards carried assault rifles and surrounded the perimeter. They approached every car with caution. As we approached the checkpoint, Mario noticed my anxiety and told us to pretend that we were asleep. Mateo did as he was told, and I shut my eyes, but the hellish gates were imprinted in my mind.

Moments later, a loud thumping on the window jolted me, and I felt Mario reach over to lower it. I squeezed my eyes shut. A deep chill filled the air, and I held my breath.

A strange deep voice spoke a mysterious language and Mario replied. I felt two arms meet in the middle of my face and slightly graze my cheek. I shuddered and squeezed my eyes shut further. Then my eyelids suddenly grew red as a light shone on my face. Someone grabbed my arms and shook me.

I opened my eyes slowly. I could barely see past the brilliance of the light, but beyond it there appeared to be a dark silhouette of what looked like a man. A shadow, darker than darkness itself. The shadow repeated itself, this time with a harsher tone.

My mouth and eyes were glued open. I let out a whimper, barely audible, that quickly dissipated into the air. The shadow spoke for a third time, much louder than before.

I barely recognized Mateo's reply as he spoke for me in that same strange language. Later I'd learn that he told the guard that I hadn't started English lessons yet.

The light quickly moved away from me and toward my brother. Mateo put his arm around me and whispered into my ear.

"He's asking you what your name is," he spoke in Spanish. I looked over to where Shadow's eyes should be.

"Pancho," I said. There was a pause that felt like an eternity before Shadow finally receded into the darkness. The Ford pulled forward and drove through the gates. I relaxed into Mateo's shoulder. Exhausted from the journey, having enough distance between the border and our new destination, I let my body succumb to sleep.

CHAPTER 4

Welcome

Papa carried my brother and me inside our new home when we finally arrived in Orange County, California.

The rest of my family made the treacherous crossing on foot. They spent a week traveling mainly by night, with help from guides called coyotes, who themselves threatened my family members' safety. They stayed with strangers in a makeshift cabin, remote and out of sight.

The coyotes did indeed act like animals. Despite many families paying in advance, the coyotes inflated their prices and forced them to pay more. Those that had no more were forced to leave, including small children who came alone from an even greater distance. Mama would recall those few weeks of staying hypervigilant, sacrificing sleep to watch over her kids and protect them from the animals hired to help them.

Eventually we all made it to Anaheim. Papa marked the success of our journey by putting Mama's crucifix in between two flags up on our dining room wall: an American flag and a Mexican flag, celebrating our new bicultural identity.

I really wish we'd ended up in a house with a white picket fence and a two-car garage, but our American dream soured into a living nightmare. We were human storage, stuffed here and there with another family in the ugliest house on the block. My siblings and I had to grow up fast, often scrimping and pooling our resources together just to get groceries. We made the small space work as best we could, and I actually enjoyed all of us snuggled into only a few beds. What mattered was that we were together. My family back home was a big source of support. They called every single day, even if they had nothing to say. My older tias would call us by phone, while my cousins would connect with us online, updating us on the latest news. In a few years, most of my cousins would go on to study in universities, and I couldn't help but hold on to a fantasy of being back home with them. Mostly I spent my days ruminating on what my life would be like had we stayed in Mexico. Accepting my reality was difficult. I would sometimes make friends in the neighborhood, but the cost of living was increasing and often my friends' families would have to move away. Thoughts crept into my head that I was unlikable, and my heart tallied all the people I had lost.

Days were harder when my siblings went to school. My parents wanted me to be able to understand English a bit more, so they decided I would wait until the next year to start school. I felt alone and would wander the neighborhood when Mama was napping. I'd walk down the street and imagine that my cousins and tias still lived only a few doors down from us. The neighborhood kids would often look away when I made eye contact. It felt like nobody wanted me there.

One day, I passed my neighbors from across the street, a young Hispanic girl named Karen and her older sister Rebecca.

Their gazes were hateful. Rebecca shadowed her eyes with a hand; the reflection of her graduation ring made me feel like I was under a spotlight.

"What are you staring at, clown?" Rebecca asked.

Karen laughed. Unsure of how to answer, I froze in place. I tried to tell her I was just walking home, but no words came out. She scanned me from head to toe. "I can't believe your parents dress you like that." Karen laughed harder. "What kind of shoes are those?" she crowed, pointing at my colorful leather huaraches. "They look like the shoes of a clown!"

I walked away, but my stride wasn't

quick enough to escape their hateful comments. They ridiculed me, called me *beaner*, *wetback*, and even commented on my weight. I couldn't understand why anyone would insult someone for things they couldn't change.

Days passed, and every afternoon I would walk to the corner to meet my siblings on their way back from school. I would hear the same words, shouted from a distance with the same hateful voices.

You're a fat clown.

Nobody wants you here.

You should have stayed on your side of the river.

I started believing their comments. Daily tasks like getting out of bed, brushing my teeth, and even showering became very difficult. Despite being hungry during the day, I wouldn't eat. In the evenings, I would overdo it, as if my body were making up for the meals it had lost. This led to feelings of shame. I would stare at myself in the mirror and hear my neighbors' comments, this time coming from inside my head.

I'm so fat.

I wish I never came here.

Nobody wants me here.

My parents knew something was wrong, and one morning I woke up to a gentle lick from a Labrador retriever puppy with limbs still too big for his small body. We named him Coaxoch, an Aztec warrior name.

Papa and I walked Coaxoch around the block, and the happy puppy followed his nose and shook his tail with every step. Papa asked about my reserved behavior, and I didn't dare tell him the truth, fearing that it would hurt his feelings. I simply told him I was still getting used to this new chapter in our life.

As if he could read my mind, my dad said, "Don't pay attention to their comments. Just do what you have to do and be better." Papa continued, "Some folks hate themselves because the world around them teaches them to," he said, "but you're allowed to exist as yourself without allowing others to pollute the air around you."

I chewed on his words, spoken as if Joselito had said them himself. They made me feel a little better. I thought about our vecinos' comments. Even though they stung, I would never be able to control what they said, so why waste effort and energy on them? I felt sorry for them, for rejecting their identity and taking it out on a boy. I decided to only worry about the things under my control.

Fighting through the darkness was tough. I often felt like a car with a dead battery, but on the worst days, when I found it the most difficult to get up or to eat, Coaxoch became the jolt that jump-started me and got me moving. We walked every day together, the pup practically pulling me across our neighborhood.

One day, I awoke and was surprised that Coaxoch hadn't licked me awake. I called to him, but he didn't come. I wondered if Mama had let him out to go to the bathroom, but she was still asleep. Stepping into the cold backyard, I sensed something was wrong. Twigs and dead grass crackled beneath my feet as I crossed the lawn. The line of ants was the first thing I noticed, leading to his still body.

My dog—my best friend—had been poisoned. He was surrounded by half-eaten hot dogs laced with something toxic. On the tall stone wall that separated our house from our neighbors', written in red paint, were the words GO HOME CLOWN.

We feared calling 911 because of our immigration status, and grieved Coaxoch's death silently. I knew then that I was also grieving the last scrap of hope I'd held for our perfect American dream. Papa took down the Mexican flag shortly after.

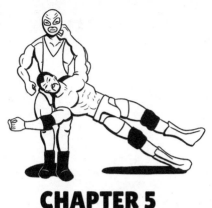

CHAPTER 5

Conflict

Time marched on and the new school year finally arrived. I was nervous but hopeful about starting school and making friends.

Mrs. Harriet's class was made up of thirty kids. She had us sit crisscross-style on the floor of her room. Her English was great: she spoke really fast, but I was able to pick up most of it. I sat toward the back of the room, crisscross on the floor, right by my teacher's sleek black metal desk, next to a spiky-haired boy with a round face. The boy's BIG DADDY COOL DIESEL truck shirt made me want to be best friends with him.

As Mrs. Harriet passed out name tags and writing utensils, she asked us to introduce ourselves and give our favorite color. The students began scribbling their names and sticking them on their navy-blue collared uniform shirts. I wrote mine down as one student started his introduction. My eyes wandered around the room, and my heart sank when I saw Karen sitting on the opposite end, her dark hair complemented with a pink bow tie. Our gazes met for an instant and she looked away.

I could still see Coaxoch's empty eyes as she dismissed me. I pressed my back against Mrs. Harriet's desk and sank deeper and deeper, until I was completely hidden under it.

"You forgot the boy under the desk," someone said a few minutes later.

I held my breath.

Mrs. Harriet ducked down, cocked her head, and raised her eyebrow.

"Lewis," she said. I tried to tell her that wasn't my name, but no words came out. Mrs. Harriet called for me a few more times before giving up and moving on with her lesson. I remained under there, listening to the classroom all around me, every comment and word whispered about the boy named Lewis, who hid under the desk. I clutched my knees to my chest and buried my head.

At ten o'clock the bell rang, and the students were excused to recess. I wiped my tears and poked my head out from under my hiding place. The classroom was empty, filled only with the faint echoes of children playing outside. There was a globe near the exit and I walked toward it. I stared at it before placing my hand on its blue and green hollow surface, surprised that my span covered many countries.

"I want to go home," I said to the empty room. I looked down at my name tag. LOO-ESE it said, to make it easier for everyone. I ripped it into little pieces and marched outside.

"I want to go home," I repeated to nobody in particular. As I crossed toward the main gates, I looked back as a crowd of students began calling out to me. I felt my face grow hot with annoyance and my pace increased.

"Hey, get back here!" someone shouted.

I quickly turned to look back. The parent-teacher coordinator came barreling toward me. Surprised at the distance she covered within a few seconds, I bolted down the street.

She called out to a nearby neighbor, a

brown-skinned woman in her early twenties working in her garden. She pounced on me and effortlessly scooped me up. I clawed at her in a vain attempt to loosen her grip, but she held me tightly from behind.

"Let me go!" I pleaded to her. "I want to go home!"

She gently shushed me. "No puedes, hijo," she spoke in Spanish. "You have to stay!"

I couldn't stop the tears as they began to fall. Later that evening, Papa and Mama tried to talk to me. They could see how upset I was.

"I wish you never brought me here," I said. They stayed quiet, and I ran out of the house.

I walked aimlessly around my neighbor-hood as the sun slowly set. As I rounded a corner on a nearby street, I saw the round-faced spiky-haired boy standing in front of a house with a stone wall. I walked over to him. He stood above a mess of pro wrestling action figures littered all over the ground. He looked up and I smiled at him.

"Hola," he said. "Me llamo Ben."

I gave him a curt nod.

"I heard you made it all the way to Garza Street." Ben spoke to me in Spanish with a slight American accent. Taking my eyes off the figures, I met his gaze.

"Not as far as I wanted to go," I replied

in English, ignoring the surprised arch of his eyebrows.

***

Hanging out with Ben at school finally made me feel okay to be myself. My hair had already been longer than most boys' hair, but I let it grow and adopted Ben's all-black attire as well as his playlists. We were inseparable, hanging out in class, during recess, and after school. We would read together, write stories, watch wrestling, and re-create our favorite matches with his action figures.

One morning Ben's mom provided us with tacos dorados. We indulged before school on the very top of a jungle gym dome. Off in the distance by the hallways I saw Karen talking to David, a brown boy with short hair who liked her. He whispered in her ear and pointed over to us.

A moment later David jogged by with a smirk painted on his face.

"Hey, beaners! Enjoying those tacos?" He pointed his hands toward us like finger guns. His grin stretched from ear to ear, as if he had just recited an amazing joke. David's statement left me speechless.

This kid is Latin American just like me.

"You're one to talk David, se te ve el nopal en la cara!" Ben yelled, calling David out on the hypocrisy of his insults.

In class later, I stood complacently, like a good soldier, with my hand over my heart, mechanically reciting the Pledge of Allegiance. But my eyes were glued to David instead of the nation's colors. He looked at me and whispered the same insult under his breath, pointing his finger guns at me with the same toothy grin. I gnawed off my eraser head and threw it at him with a wild swing. The rubber nib bounced off his forehead.

"Lewis!" Mrs. Harriet yelled, mispronouncing my name yet again. "You don't horse around during the Pledge of Allegiance. You know this!"

"He keeps calling me *beaner*." I struggled

to let the words out. Mrs. Harriet turned her attention to David.

"David, stop saying mean things to your peers, you understand?"

That's it? This boy called me a racist word and that's all she has to say?

"Sorry, *Lewis*," David mocked.

After school, in the parking lot, I encountered David again. Karen whispered into his ear, and this time he called me a clown and pointed his finger guns. I couldn't restrain myself and I swung my right arm awkwardly, hitting him in the stomach. David grabbed my hair and folded my hoodie over my head in retaliation. He took hold of my backpack and swung me, throwing me straight into the chain-link fence. I felt a sharp pain in my forehead and ignored the warm liquid slowly rolling down my face.

I heard a crowd of boys whoop in excitement, and Ben yelled at David to fight fair. I removed my backpack and hoodie, tossing them onto the pavement. I charged into him head down and tackled him, landing right on top. David drove his thumbs into my eye sockets, and I squinted hard in defense.

A moment later, my shirt grew tight around my neck as David's mother hauled me off of him. The crowd dispersed, and I came face-to-face with Mr. Russel and Mr. Winston, two teachers with furrowed brows and intensity in their eyes. David and his mom scurried off as the two teachers strode toward me and dragged me away.

They didn't believe me that David and Karen were calling me derogatory names, and I was blamed for the entire fight. I was suspended and forced into a different class.

I felt awful that I was separated from Ben. The new classroom didn't offer respite from hateful comments.

I grew angry with my parents and blamed them.

You said you'd protect me.

I didn't hear Joselito's voice.

**

Still resentful of my parents for bringing me to the States, I went to speak to my brother Mateo. He listened to me and started taking me to a community club wrestling practice the next day.

I'd never seen that side of my brother before. He was so agile, strong, and admired by his teammates. He went by Mathew there and everyone on Team eXcel seemed to care what he had to say. On top of that, Coach McCarthy was a fair man, treating everyone with respect.

I joined the team and was often paired with a ninth-grade blonde girl named Tiffany. I grew to like her and would always shower and do my hair before practice. Mateo would laugh. I asked him once if he thought I had a shot with an American girl. Despite the huge age gap between Tiffany and me, my brother filled me with confidence as always.

One day I was drilling with Tiffany, trying to find the courage to ask her out. She asked if my brother was single, and I grew envious. I saw all his friends in practice and became resentful. I blamed him that I couldn't make friends of my own, that I didn't have class with Ben anymore, that I was brought to the States and didn't fit in. I hated him because all our teammates in Team eXcel referred to me as "Lil Mathew."

My heart grew so filled with rage, and I was so angry at my siblings and caregivers, that I actually prayed for my brother Mateo to suffer.

But I continued to attend practice, and after a few months of training, I started feeling more confident in school. One day during recess, in the middle of an intense game of handball, David and Karen sat on some wooden benches in front of me. I looked at them curiously.

"Let's just play," said Ben, hoping I'd dismiss them.

"It's all good," I replied, surprised at the steadiness of my own voice as I tried not to shake. I locked eyes with Karen as she whispered in her lackey's ear and handed him a small gleaming object. David grinned and walked over to me, slipping on what I finally saw was a fat golden ring. He made a fist and Ben sighed.

" 'Sup, beaners," he said. "How 'bout a little game of bloody knuckles?" I looked down at the graduation ring. Rebecca's, I presumed. "I bet you can't last three rounds with me."

"I'll play you three rounds," I said, "if you play another game with me after."

David glanced at Ben holding the handball and smiled. "Okay," he said. "I'll go first."

I made a fist, raised my arm to chest-level, and took a deep breath. David swung. The impact of the ring crushing into my knuckles shook me. I swallowed a scream and bit the inside of my mouth, refusing to wear the pain on my face. In my mind, I heard coach McCarthy's voice tell me to never show my opponent I was hurting. I looked at David, his eyes slightly wide in surprise.

"Mercy?" David's voice came out as a whisper, asking if I wanted to give up, but I shook my head and gently raised his ring hand up. I aimed at his pinkie, away from the golden object on his middle finger, and swung hard. My fist collided head-on with the smaller digits of his hand. My hand ached at the blow, and I felt a jolt shoot through my body. My poker face remained. I glanced at him and thought I saw his brow furrow.

"Mercy?" I asked, ignoring the intense pain in my hand. David bit his lower lip and shook his head.

We went like that, our knuckles bleeding and swollen, a crowd gathering around us, until David went in for his final round. He swung with his entire body, but the ring scraped the fat of my hand, missing my knuckles completely. The crowd erupted.

David shook his head and laughed in embarrassment. Feeling relieved, I raised my mangled fist and gently knocked on his knuckles, for my final turn. David bit his lip and frowned.

"Ready to play something else?" I asked. David stared, lowering his battered fist. I removed my school shirt and revealed the tighter shirt I wore underneath. I could almost feel him reading the black and gold words: MAGNOLIA WRESTLING: TEAM EXCEL.

"You wanna wrestle?" I asked. Karen's jaw dropped just as the bell went off, signaling the end of recess. Neither of them bothered me again.

***

Later that night, I awoke to a thumping on my window. I called out to Mateo, but he wasn't in his bed across our room. I crept into the hallway and felt the chill air of the night seeping into our living room. The door was wide open, and I could hear footsteps.

Had someone broken in?

The footsteps approached, and I held my breath, fearing the worst. Mateo walked in, looking dazed. I called out to him, but nothing indicated that he heard me. Something was wrong.

I walked up to my brother and shuddered when I looked him in the eyes. His gaze was empty and haunted. Whoever this was, was not my brother. I thought about the nagual, a shape-shifting creature of Mexican folklore. His eyes focused a moment later, and I finally recognized him.

"I'm scared," he told me. "The voices, they won't stop."

My stomach turned over, but I took Mateo by the arm and led him into our room. He asked if we could put our beds side by side for the night. I remember feeling stunned—Mateo was one of the bravest and strongest people I knew. How could he, of all people, be scared? Had I done this when I'd prayed for him to suffer?

I fought off the guilt and I pushed our beds together. I put on AC/DC's *Fly on the Wall*. I watched him until he fell asleep, still not sure if he was a shape-shifter or not.

CHAPTER 6

Distortion

A few years passed, and our family went through thick and thin together. Isabel and Hector finished high school and started working to help our parents carry the financial burden.

Mateo, however, continued to act really bizarre.

He went out one evening when I was ten and came home around three a.m. I was worried sick waiting for him. When I asked where he was, he said he was looking for Lestat, a vampire from the Anne Rice books.

The following night, I awoke to a strange sound. When I looked around, I noticed Mateo was gone. The front door was wide open. I hurried outside and saw my brother turning the corner at the end of the block. I sprinted after him, surprised at how fast I was moving, but I still couldn't catch him. I wandered the streets for what seemed like an eternity, unsure of where he had gone. I figured it was best to go home and wake Joanna. On my way back, just a few blocks shy of my house, a red and blue beacon lit up the sky. My brother stood in between three squad cars and was surrounded by six officers.

"Get down on the ground!" one shouted.

"Put your hands up!" demanded another.

"On your knees!" yelled another voice.

My brother froze with all the conflicting commands. The officers threw themselves at Mateo, quickly flattening him. I gasped, feeling small and helpless. I ran behind a nearby bush and listened. I heard shouts from the men to hold him down, to cuff him. I wanted to help, but I was paralyzed, and I clutched my knees to my chest. My brother's screams of pain echoed throughout the streets. He yelled, pleaded for help, and begged them to stop.

I ran.

My siblings and I all stayed awake that night. An officer called us an hour later and asked for Mateo's address, citizenship status, and other info. The officer hung up on us without a single word after we gave him what he wanted. Our family was scared. We were unsure whether we would see Mateo ever again. We were certain he would get deported. Two sleepless nights later, around three a.m., we heard a gentle knock on the door. Mateo walked in, the same lost look in his eyes. We all embraced him, relieved to be together again, but a foreboding feeling spread into our hearts. Something was still off about Mateo.

**

"The nagual," I whimpered, trying to make sense of the chaos in front of me.

I looked at Mateo, or someone who looked like him, as he tore up our furniture with inhuman strength. He smashed chairs effortlessly. He dragged cabinets across the floor and sent them barreling. He lifted my bed as if it were weightless and threw it through our back window, where it smashed on the concrete patio. Blood ran down from his broad back and forearms, and I was surprised to see it was red. My brain tried to grasp just what I was seeing, thinking of every possible explanation. I thought about how I'd prayed for my brother's harm, and my guilty conscience flared up. I shook it off and got mad at him instead.

You were supposed to protect me.

Don't leave me.

This is all my fault.

Everyone was scared and cowered out of his way. We looked at Papa for answers and he told us to just let Mateo tire himself out. Time crawled forward. It seemed interminable.

Just when it seemed like he had destroyed everything, Mateo heaved Mama's crucifix off the dining room wall, and my gut turned over. He lumbered out to the front yard and we all followed in stunned silence. He swung it onto the sidewalk, and it splintered into pieces. Our final heirloom of Mexico was gone in an instant. Mama finally gave the command and Papa and Hector grabbed Mateo from behind, pulling him back inside.

Eventually, Mateo calmed down. He sat in the darkness of our barren room scribbling on himself and all over the walls.

Emergency Medical Services arrived ten minutes later and took him away.

A few days later I overheard my parents talking about Mateo. He had seen a doctor, one for your mind. They told them he had a sickness. An illness of the soul that makes people lose touch with reality, often causing them to see or hear things that aren't there. I clenched my fist when I heard that he would never be the same. My soul cracked under the guilt, convinced that I was to blame. But it was easier to push that anger outward.

In my mind, my brother had left me. When Mateo finally came home, Mama cried almost every night. She blamed herself. Papa thought it was drug use and asked his friends not to visit anymore, opting to blame them for everything.

Mateo seemed so different under medication. Sometimes it seemed like his soul would leave his body and he would zone out. When he was alert, he acted like a child with no social skills and would react to things that weren't really there. I was so upset with him; his transition was so sudden and so severe. Deep down, I knew he was sick, but it felt like he had run through the door of his imagination and slammed it shut, and I hated him for leaving me.

You were supposed to protect me.

You were supposed to keep me grounded.

What do I do without you?

**

My family was evicted from our house shortly after the attacks on the World Trade Center. In the months following that terrorist attack on America, hate crimes rose against Arabs, Muslims, and persons perceived as members of those groups, including my family. On his way home from work as a hotel banquet server, Papa had been targeted and attacked, presumed to be Muslim. He'd come home badly beaten, dripping in blood. It was the first time I saw him cry. The injuries left him unable to work for a few months, causing us to miss our rent payments. Our landlord told us to get out immediately, even threatening to call immigration enforcement on us. The instability of our environment, and these out-of-control situations, made me mistrust my parents and siblings. I became angry and reserved and I blamed them for all that was happening. With no place else to go, we bounced around from motel to motel. I'd share a room with Mateo and I grew more resentful due to his unpredictability.

One night, he walked up to me while I

was lying in bed and spat on me. I grabbed him by the neck and socked him across the face.

"I'm sorry," he said. "The voices told me to do it."

"I hate you," I yelled, and continued to hit him. "You're not my brother. My brother died. You're a wretch of a human being."

Mama had woken up and hurried between us, begging me to stop hitting him. I felt so betrayed by my family that they'd allow my brother to get sick and allow us to live under those conditions. It was like a switch flipped deep down inside me. I became self-obsessed with my own preservation, and my compassion for my family started to dwindle.

I felt as if I were owed the world. And whatever I wanted, I took.

CHAPTER 7

Catharsis

Middle school was a big change and I struggled to adapt. I didn't feel comfortable going to teachers for emotional support. I felt like a burden, so I often skipped class, and my grades suffered.

I got the news that I would be held back if I failed summer school. I thought about losing my friend Ben, one of the only positive parts of my life. I attended seventh-grade summer math with my back against the wall, but I felt a glint of hope when I saw my teacher.

Coach McCarthy hadn't changed much since the last time I saw him. He still wore the same beige collared shirt, tucked into his loose dress shorts. We made eye contact but he looked away, no sign that he recognized me. My thoughts yelled that I was unimportant. He went down the role sheet and I held my breath.

Please look at me.

Recognize me.

Help me.

"Lewis On-fire," he called out.

Is this guy serious? I thought, feeling insignificant. Forgettable. He called out again. I laid my head down and raised my hand, defeated.

McCarthy went through the syllabus, describing not only the subject matter expected, but also his three-absences-and-you're-out policy. I stared a hole through him.

After school, when I arrived at our new apartment a few suburbs away, my sister Isabel was in the living room getting ready for work. She took the lead in trying to take care of our family, since the language barrier my parents faced made it difficult for them to do so. I aggressively asked if she had found us a place to live, closer to my school and friend. She didn't react, which was a bad sign. She was taking on a lot for us, but it was hard to feel grateful.

Isabel didn't come home from work that night.

We spent the morning looking for her. I scouted West Anaheim where we used to live. I felt bad for missing class, and for not feeling more concern for my sister. By luck I took a shortcut through a random laundromat parking lot and found her red Honda unlocked, the keys still in the ignition.

I called Joanna on a pay phone and let her

know I had Isabel's car. Joanna told me our eldest sister had finally come home, though something was wrong with her. She told me Isabel was not herself and was acting really strangely. In addition, she had donated all her stuff to the local Goodwill. The pressure of taking care of our family had been too much for her.

Worry gnawed at me, my brother's face flashing through my mind. I shuddered at the thought of my sister getting sick, but stuffed down the feelings and chose to be angry at the inconvenience instead.

During the fourth week of summer school, our new apartment was being fumigated and Papa had arranged for us to stay in the hotel where he was employed. I was looking forward to the shorter bus ride to school, perhaps exploring the hotel and reading by the pool.

On our first and only evening there, while the rest of the family was out running errands or working, Mateo was pacing back and forth in our room. Mama had asked me to help watch him, but he was irritating me.

"Let's go outside," I commanded, and he followed.

The pool was closed, so I sat on the patio furniture reading Dean Koontz, while my brother stood a few feet away from me.

I watched him bobbing his head, lost in his thoughts, and pushed down the feelings of guilt.

"You wretch," I muttered to myself. In my peripheral vision, I caught a glimpse of a middle-aged white woman carrying shopping bags and walking toward the glass doors behind me.

"Thanks for the help," she sarcastically stated as she passed through. She gave me a cold, hateful glare and I locked gazes with her, reciprocating.

"You're welcome," I retorted.

A few hours later, Papa arrived at our rooms still in his work attire. He told us to pack up our belongings; we were being kicked out. Shocked, I asked why, and he told us that several tourists complained about two suspicious guests causing "disturbances."

I pleaded with Papa, as if that could help. I told him that I was just reading and Mateo was just standing by me. I begged him to check the security cameras. In his eyes, I could see that he believed me, but with his job on the line he had to fall in line and be complacent.

I almost laughed at the prejudice, at how reality was distorted; at how two boys, behaving lawfully, were quickly labeled as dangerous, as suspicious. I was overcome with anger, at the cruelty of that woman, of the hotel. They didn't care that we had nowhere else to go. I felt injustice on my brother's behalf, but quickly tucked the feeling away, preferring to remain angry at my father. At my brother, the wretch. That night we slept in our vehicles, and the next day I missed my second day of summer school.

I continued to attend math class, struggling but failing to ask for help. During week eight, I got the flu but continued attending, in defiance of getting left behind.

On the last day of class, still suffering from the aftereffects of the flu, McCarthy called us all up to speak with him individually about our final grades. Before the final, I'd been close to failing with a low D. If I didn't get a C in the class, I would be stuck in middle school for an extra year.

He went down the role sheet alphabetically, excusing students for the day after he spoke with them. He skipped me.

I grew more and more confused as he went further and away from my name. Part of me hoped he still recognized me and was waiting to speak to me until the end. But I knew deep down that I hadn't done well enough on the final to raise my grade.

"All right, sick boy," he said, "your turn."

I rolled my eyes, walked over, and sank down on the seat in front of him.

"Listen," he said, pausing to look at me. "That's quite the glare you have." I ignored him, and he continued. "I just graded your final exam, and though you did pretty well, your grade is still under the C needed to pa—"

Not wanting to hear more, I stormed out the door. I walked until I found myself in the school's wrestling room. On the far wall, the famous "30 Wins Club" was painted in gold, with names that went all the way back to the 1960s. A boy named Herb held the record of 50 wins in 1973. My brother was the closest, with 36. I traced the outline of his name with my finger, forcing my bottom lip to stop quivering.

"You look just like your brother, you know."

I froze.

"I was gutted when I heard what happened to him."

Was this guy just messing with me?

I turned around and saw McCarthy in the doorway, smiling. I was relieved to be seen, to be recognized.

McCarthy asked me what I wanted to be when I grew up, a question I'd hated ever since elementary school.

I kept silent. I hated talking about myself. I didn't trust anyone and I wasn't going to open up to him.

"I was like you once," he said, as if he could see right through me. "I tried to wear a mask to protect myself, but I quickly found out it wasn't even like being alive."

He seemed genuine and sincere, perhaps the best teacher I had up to this point.

"What does it matter?" I asked quietly. "No one thinks I'm going to do anything with my life anyway."

I felt a pain in the pit of my stomach, as if I were falling. He sat with me for a few minutes in silence and finally spoke. "You can be whatever you want."

"Not in this country," I snapped back at him. "Land of opportunity, sure. My life was fine before I was dragged to this miserable place."

He laughed. *Laughed.* Insufferable man.

"You've been carrying that grudge this entire time, huh?" He said. "I understand you feel like you're owed the world, but you really have a lot to be grateful for. You have a family that loves and supports you unconditionally."

He was right, and I hated him for it.

McCarthy sighed and pulled a mirror off his file cabinet. He pointed at the mirror on the wall. I struggled to make eye contact with my reflection. I felt unworthy and unlovable.

"What do you see?" he asked me. I was confused by the question.

"Listen, I know about your family's story. Mathew didn't fill me in on all the details and I'll never know how hard it is to leave everything you know behind, but the past is the past. Your family brought you here, they gambled and risked their lives. What do you see?" he repeated. "Do you see a victim, or do you see a survivor?"

I made eye contact with myself and felt an unknown weight I was carrying slide off my chest. I heard a voice off in the distance. What was his name? Joselito. The saint hero of my hometown. The boy that mothers would ask to help reframe their child's inner negative thoughts.

"Your grades can't take you far right now, the route you're heading. But I'll pass you *if* you come to one practice when you're in high school. I see how tough you are, powering through even with a fever. Utilize that and reclaim your life.

But it starts here. Wrestle for me and get a scholarship. Get an education. Make something of yourself."

"You'll pass me if I just show up to one wrestling practice?" I asked, hesitating. It sounded too good to be true.

"Yes," he replied. We shook hands. As I left the room, I turned around and pointed at the 30 Wins Club.

"I'm going to break that record," I said.

McCarthy smiled. "See you at practice."

**

As I walked toward the bus that day, the oppressive feeling that used to coat me seemed to have evaporated. I didn't mind the hour-long bus ride and felt happy when I arrived at the apartment, our home. I saw Mateo playing guitar in the corner. I looked at him, and he turned toward me and smiled shyly. My brother, the boy who had backed me up at the border and taught me so many life lessons. The person who gave me confidence in myself. Who kept me grounded. Who lifted my spirits when I was at my lowest.

What was I even doing?

He's your brother.

I heard the voice of Joselito again. I felt a shame so overwhelming I almost crumpled.

"Mateo," I whispered softly, and watched him react.

He's still in there.
He's your brother.

His eyes fluttered about, looking over at me cautiously, perhaps unsure of which terrible treatment I'd give him this time. I took his arm gently, hearing the voice whisper in my mind:

You can be whatever you want.

I looked at my brother for the first time in a long time, accepting the illness that he was suffering from. I felt like I knew my purpose.

I'm a survivor.

Wrestle.

Get an education.

Learn about mental illness.

Help my brother.

"I'm going to help you, bro," I told him. He smiled at me.

"Want to listen to *Fly on the Wall*?" he asked.

We did.

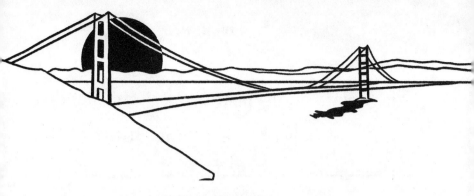

EPILOGUE

Connection

February 2022, 04:00

San Francisco, CA

Our unit, Street Crisis Unit 1, tells the 911 dispatch team that we are active and ready to take calls. We patrol the Bayview, a neighborhood in the lower east part of San Francisco. My paramedic for the morning is Avelar and my peer counselor is Samory. Both work with me in the Street Crisis Response Team (SCRT), an alternative to law enforcement in which a peer counselor with lived experience, a community paramedic, and a mental health professional are dispatched to behavioral-health-related 911 calls. I am very proud to be a part of this new mission that prioritizes mental health, something near and dear to me.

Funded by the city of San Francisco, SCRT was designed in response to the murder of George Floyd, whose death was a recent one in a long line of murders caused by excessive police violence against people of color. I think back to my childhood, and my brother, and all the officers shouting different orders.

Our dispatch buzzer goes off, signaling that we have a call. The radio describes a Black woman on a bus refusing to get off.

"Copy," Avelar says. "Street Crisis One en route."

We arrive on scene in West Portal. Armed police officers surround the outside of bus 24.

"She's inside," one officer says, pointing toward the idle bus. Through the window, I see a Black woman sitting in the back with four officers towering over her. We board the bus just as one officer starts losing his patience, grabbing the woman's arm and attempting to drag her out with force. The woman retaliates and slaps at the cop's grip. I can see the three other cops tense.

"There's no need for that, Officers," Samory says assertively, causing them to back up.

"Thank you, Samory," I tell him.

"I gotchu, bro," he replies.

Avelar escorts the officers off the bus and then we get to work. The woman sits still in the backseat with her eyes shut: she's pretending to be asleep.

"Good morning, ma'am," I say as I sit a few seats from her. Samory sits across the aisle. "My name is Luis," I say. "I'm a therapist with Street Crisis. What's your name?"

She doesn't respond. I hear an officer shout from outside that we're wasting time.

"Be patient," Avelar says to them.

"Ma'am, the police are gone, it's just us now." I ask the woman for permission to touch her wrist. She doesn't reply, but she doesn't resist, either.

"Okay, ma'am, I'm going to reach for your wrist now, all right?" I gently grab hold of her. She helps me by turning her arm. I pull up her sleeve and find a wristband from a hospital. I read her name and make a note of her date of birth.

"What a lovely name," I tell her. I make small talk and the woman replies every so often. She tells me about herself and I make her feel heard. Samory brings her food and some coffee. Street Crisis rigs usually don't have coffee in them, but we get up extra-early to brew some for our early morning calls. The woman happily accepts the brew and Avelar puts a blanket around her back. She willingly walks off the bus with us, and we are greeted by a chorus of applause from San Francisco's police.

Crisis averted: Another person has been saved from excessive police force. Now the real work begins. We eventually find the woman a stabilization program, in which she is offered housing for a few weeks. We add her to a list of people who need follow-up appointments to receive a phone and connect with General Assistance and any other resources needs.

**

I finish counting to fifteen silently in my head and lean my body to one side, stretching my hamstrings and quad muscles in preparation for my self-care to balance a long work week, one of the rougher ones during my time with SCRT. My dog Sombra waits patiently beside me, sniffing the flowers that freshly sprouted at McClaren Park.

I begin my run and Sombra follows closely behind. As I focus on the sound of my footsteps, I acknowledge the small victory of running outside after work. It would have been easy to justify staying in and not taking care of myself, but since I've grown, so has my insight into my unhealthy patterns of coping and the path they could encourage.

I make my way through McClaren. The work week flows through my mind, and I see the faces of every patient during every mental-health-related crisis call. I run past trees and control my breathing, inhaling through my nose and exhaling through my mouth, and think about the woman on the bus, my sense of relief as we were able to escort her out safely. I begin my ascent up the incline of the park as more calls flow through my head. They metabolize through my body, get processed and get stored away into memories.

I finally arrive at the top of Mansell Heights and scan the horizon, admiring the view. Off in the distance, I can see the Port of Oakland cranes and the whole San Francisco Peninsula. I linger in the moment and scan south, beyond California, toward Michoacán. I feel at peace, no longer shackled by grudges, resentment, and what-if fantasies. My thoughts go to my home, my parents, my siblings, and our sacrifice. I think about the path I've walked, and the souls that have come and gone along the way, many leaving tally marks on my heart. In the past, I saw them as having abandoned me, though now I can see them for what they really were: stray beams of light that were my beacon for a little while. The scars became stars in the sky, a constellation I can always see and carry with me. Though my story of migration had a beginning and an ending, I know my journey of mental health is a never-ending one. One that continues onward, each and every day.

Continue the Discussion

How did crossing the border impact Luis's life?

Luis crossed the border during a vital part of growing up. With so many factors out of his control in his environment and so many people coming and going, Luis became untrusting of his parents and siblings. Losing trust in caregivers can lead to someone feeling suspicious of others. Being in between two cultures, Luis struggled with identity issues. On top of that, he often felt like a burden to everyone around him, had difficulty liking himself and even had recurrent thoughts of hurting himself. Luis struggled with depression and stress in his life. He often felt alone and was afraid of abandonment. But with hard work and therapy, he made progress to undo lots of unseen childhood wounds.

Why do some people choose to cross the southern border of the United States?

The truth of the matter is that sometimes people don't choose to cross the border—they simply don't have the choice not to cross it. Many people cross into the United States seeking asylum, or safety from violence, in a new land. However, most folks, like Luis's family, migrate for financial opportunities, or to start fresh.

What are some challenges that children who have migrated from Mexico to the United States face?

Children who migrate from Mexico to the United States can struggle with identity issues, such as being filtered out as "too white" for their own culture, but "too brown" for their new culture. This can lead to internalized racism, or a rejection of their identity and roots.

The journey itself is very treacherous

and dangerous. Children are often killed or die for other reasons during the journey, such as from exposure to the elements. They can be separated from their families or can fall victim to sexual or physical abuse. Once they arrive in the United States, children can be subject to prejudice and racism.

How can you, as a family member or friend, help somebody who is going through a mental health crisis?

You can do several things to help. These include:

1. Learning more about the mental illness.
2. Listening to and validating your loved one.
3. Asking how you can help them, and respecting their choices as long as they are not at risk.
4. Staying connected.
5. Helping them make a crisis plan, and providing options for other ways they can get support.
6. Encouraging them to continue their treatment plan, and offering them support with incremental goals.

What is Luis doing now?

Luis is working as a mental health therapist with crisis and school-based services in California. Luis coaches wrestling at a local college. In the summer, Luis travels back to Michoacán and offers free mental health support services to his vecinos from his hometown. In his free time, Luis writes creatively.

Get Involved

1. Be mindful, think inwardly.

Mindfulness focuses on purposely being aware of the present moment, acknowledging thoughts but not allowing them to influence your behavior or reactions. Mindfulness means being open and intentional with what we do. Self-awareness is a key component in helping others. Before we can help someone else, we must be aware of our own biases and triggers to bring about a nonjudgmental presence.

2. Think globally, act locally.

With so many broad topics covered in this book, from mental health to immigrant rights to prejudice, it is easy to feel lost in that complexity. One tip for getting involved is to think globally and act locally. That means to consider the big picture and everyone and everything possibly involved, and then focus your efforts on a small, manageable scale. Work with what you've got. Examples of this include voting when you are old enough to do so, writing to elected officials, speaking up when you see an injustice, and donating to local nonprofits.

3. Consider your own mental health.

The interesting thing about therapy is that it works for many people. Though it is a lot of hard work, building emotional skills and processing trauma can help people move forward after devastating events. Admitting that you need additional support and seeking it are incredibly brave steps to take toward your own ability to make change in the world.

**Engagement guide available.
Find out more at
wwnorton.com/i-witness-series**

Timeline

1970

Luis's father, Ramon, migrates to the north to work in agriculture, returns to Michoacán shortly after because he misses his girlfriend and childhood sweetheart, Amalia.

1977

Ramon and Amalia marry.

1978

The two migrate to the United States.

1979

Amalia and Ramon have their firstborn child, Isabel.

1981

Hector is born, their second child.

1983

The family returns to Michoacán.

1985-1989

Amalia and Ramon have their third, fourth, and fifth children. Joanna, Mateo, and Luis are born.

1993

Ramon goes to the United States for a third time, leaving for California.

1994

The Mexican peso devalues three decimal points, causing a mass exodus and migration.

1996

Luis and his family journey to the United States.

2001

September 11 causes racial tensions. Millions are affected.

2007

Luis graduates from high school.

2008

Amalia becomes a U.S. citizen.

2009

Luis earns All-American honors through Santa Ana College wrestling.

2017

Luis receives his undergraduate degree, with a major in fine arts and cinema.

2019

Luis graduates again, with a master's in counseling and clinical mental health.

2023

Luis becomes a U.S. citizen.

Author's Acknowledgments

Thank you to Moncho, Mayo, Cris, and Dario. Thank you to my siblings for your unmatched patience and for allowing me to be a child a little longer. To Papa and Mama for your sacrifice. To my family back home who only knew me through pictures but always sent unconditional love and support. Thank you Coaches John McCarthy and Vince Silva. Thank you to Amanda Uhle and to Kristin Allard and the team at Norton Young Readers.

To my stray beam of light.

Editors' Acknowledgments

The editors would like to extend special thanks to the Young Editors Project (YEP), which connects young readers to manuscripts in progress. The program gives meaningful opportunities for young people to be part of the professional publishing process and gives authors and publishers thoughtful insights into their work. Special thanks to Eileen O'Mahony from Maspeth, New York; Elena Garcia Sheridan from Dudenin, New Zealand; Lily Team from Carlsbad, California; Corinne Licardo from New York, New York; Xenia Masson from Bath, England; Jordan Myaers from

Brooklyn, New York; Henry Martin from Elsah, Illinois; Will Seery from Mountain Lakes, New Jersey; and Rowan William Keel from Chicago, Illinois. We are also grateful for kind and expert guidance from Claire Astrow, Hannah Rose Neuhauser, Kristin Allard, Simon Boughton, and Anika Hussain.

www.youngeditorsproject.org

About I, Witness

I, Witness is a nonfiction book series that tells important stories of real young people who have faced and conquered extraordinary contemporary challenges. There's no better way for young readers to learn about the world's issues and upheavals than through the eyes of young people who have lived through these times.

Proceeds from this book series support the work of the International Alliance of Youth Writing Centers and its sixty-plus member organizations. These nonprofit writing centers are joined in a common belief that young people need places where they can write and be heard, where they can have their voices celebrated and amplified.

www.youthwriting.org